F.
BIBLE STUDYGUIDES

Wisdom for Today's Woman

INSIGHTS FROM ESTHER

BY POPPY SMITH

Wisdom for Today's Woman

PUBLISHED BY WATERBROOK PRESS

12265 Oracle Blvd., Suite 200

Colorado Springs, Colorado 80921

A division of Random House, Inc.

All Scripture quotations, unless otherwise indicated, are taken from the
Holy Bible, New International Version®. NIV®. Copyright © 1973, 1978, 1984
by International Bible Society. Used by permission of Zondervan Publishing
House. All rights reserved.

ISBN 0-87788-067-0

Copyright © 1998, 2001 by Patricia Smith

All rights reserved. No part of this book may be reproduced or transmitted
in any form or by any means, electronic or mechanical, including photocopying
and recording, or by any information storage and retrieval system, without
permission in writing from the publisher.

Printed in the United States of America

2005

10 9 8 7 6

Contents

Welcome to the Women of the Word Series

BY RUTH HALEY BARTON

elcome to the Women of the Word studyguides—a series especially designed to encourage women in their spiritual journey. No matter what season of life we may be in or how long we have followed Christ, we all face similar issues as women in today's world. Discovering who we are, living in relationship with others, choosing a vocational path, satisfying our spiritual hunger—we women face an unprecedented array of options. At times we are exhilarated by the opportunities, running enthusiastically from option to option like shoppers in a brand-new superstore. At other times we are confused and desperate for guidance—almost paralyzed by a panoply of choices far beyond what women in previous generations could have imagined. We need wisdom that speaks to the complexity of our lives.

Perhaps even deeper than our need for "answers" to life's questions is the desire for an intimate encounter with God. We long for a fresh expression of God's loving concern for us, a sense of personal attention in the midst of an alarmingly impersonal world. And so we approach the Scriptures with high hopes. We know that the Bible is a book like no other—God-breathed not only at the time of its initial writing but also alive and active in the present moment (Hebrews 4:12). Yet we're not always sure how to access it for ourselves. We might wonder, "Will I really have a life-giving encounter with God through the words on these pages, or is that a privilege reserved for others? How do *I* receive the life-changing power that is present in this ancient text?"

One concrete and effective way to open ourselves up to God's work in our lives is through inductive Bible study. This approach involves a dynamic interplay between the mind and the heart. First we engage our minds to read and unravel the meaning of the text. Through careful study and thought, we consider the historical context, explore the meaning of words, concepts, and principles, and reflect on what these might have meant to the original listeners. But the task of observing and interpreting information about the text is just the beginning. It is the "front porch" that leads into the "main house" of our relationship with God. No matter how nice a front porch is, we don't want to stay there forever. We want to be invited to come inside, to get comfortable, to share food and fellowship with the Master of the house. Inductive Bible study offers us just such an invitation—to engage not only our minds but also our hearts as we listen for God's Word for us today.

Our spiritual companions on this journey include the ancient women of the Bible, whose lives bear striking similarities to our own: single women making choices about relationships and lifestyle; young mothers trying to figure out how to balance love for children with other life callings; married women wrestling with the joys and the challenges of long-term commitment; women learning how to answer God's call to service and leadership in the church, the marketplace, and the global community. Regardless of differences in historical and cultural settings, their experiences and life lessons, their successes and failures speak powerfully to our own. Like us, they harbored deep and perhaps inexpressible desires for a life-transforming connection with God. Their lives demonstrate that the God who cared for a slave girl and her baby in the wilderness, answered an infertile woman's prayer, granted wisdom, political savvy, and protection to a Hebrew beauty queen, and extended loving, human touch to women who had looked for love in all the wrong places is the same God who reaches for relationship with us today.

All Scripture, including the stories of those women who have gone before, is given for our instruction, inspiration, and spiritual formation (2 Timothy 3:16). The Women of the Word studyguide series offers you a powerful tool for engaging the Scriptures for spiritual transformation. As you embark on this study, I encourage you to engage your *mind* by being disciplined in your study of historical context, biblical language, and concepts through the notes provided and other trustworthy study materials that you might have on hand. I also encourage you to engage your *imagination* as you reflect on what the biblical teachings might have meant to the women who first heard them. But don't stop there! Take the most courageous step of all by engaging your *heart* and making it your top priority to listen for *God's word to you* in the present moment.

Each time you open God's Word begin with a quiet prayer: "Speak, Lord, for your servant is listening." Trust that he will speak and then, when he does, listen and respond with increasing faithfulness so that you become a woman whose life and character are shaped by the Word.

How to Use This Studyguide

*F*isherman studyguides are based on the inductive approach to Bible study. Inductive study is discovery study; we discover what the Bible says as we ask questions about its content and search for answers. This is quite different from the process in which a teacher *tells* a group *about* the Bible—what it means and what to do about it. In inductive study God speaks directly to each of us through his Word.

A group functions best when a leader keeps the discussion on target, but the leader is neither the teacher nor the "answer person." A leader's responsibility is to *ask*—not *tell*. The answers come from the text itself as group members examine, discuss, and think together about the passage.

There are four kinds of questions in each study. The first is an *approach question.* Asked and answered before the Bible passage is read, this question breaks the ice and helps you start thinking about the topic of the Bible study. It begins to reveal where thoughts and feelings need to be transformed by Scripture.

Some of the early questions in each study are *observation questions*—who, what, where, when, and how—designed to help you learn some basic facts about the passage of Scripture.

Once you know what the Bible says, you then need to ask, *What does it mean?* These *interpretation questions* help you to discover the writer's basic message.

Next come *application questions,* which ask, *What does it mean to me?* They challenge you to live out the Scripture's life-transforming message.

Fisherman studyguides provide spaces between questions for jotting down responses as well as any related questions you would like to raise in the group. Each group member should have a copy of the studyguide and may take a turn in leading the group.

A group should use any accurate, modern translation of the Bible such as the *New International Version,* the *New American Standard Bible,* the *New Revised Standard Version,* the *New Jerusalem Bible,* or the *Good News Bible.* (Other translations or paraphrases of the Bible may be referred to when additional help is needed.) Bible commentaries should not be brought to a Bible study because they tend to dampen discussion and keep people from thinking for themselves.

SUGGESTIONS FOR GROUP LEADERS

1. Thoroughly read and study the Bible passage before the meeting. Get a firm grasp on its themes and begin applying its teachings for yourself. Pray that the Holy Spirit will "guide you into all truth" (John 16:13) so that your leadership will guide others.

2. If any of the studyguide's questions seem ambiguous or unnatural to you, rephrase them, feeling free to add others that seem necessary to bring out the meaning of a verse.

3. Begin (and end) the study promptly. Start by asking someone to pray for every participant to both understand the passage and be open to its transforming power. Remember, the Holy Spirit is the teacher, not you!

4. Ask for volunteers to read the passages aloud.

5. As you ask the studyguide's questions in sequence, encourage everyone to participate in the discussion. If some are silent, try gently suggesting, "Let's have an answer from someone who hasn't spoken up yet."

6. If a question comes up that you can't answer, don't be afraid to admit that you're baffled. Assign the topic as a research project for someone to report on next week, or say, "I'll do some studying and let you know what I find out."

7. Keep the discussion moving, but be sure it stays focused. Though a certain number of tangents are inevitable, you'll want to quickly bring the discussion back to the topic at hand. Also, learn to pace the discussion so that you finish the lesson in the time allotted.

8. Don't be afraid of silences; some questions take time to answer and some people need time to gather courage to speak. If silence persists, rephrase your question, but resist the temptation to answer it yourself.

9. If someone comes up with an answer that is clearly illogical or unbiblical, ask her for further clarification: "What verse suggests that to you?"

10. Discourage overuse of cross-references. Learn all you can from the passage at hand, while selectively incorporating a few important references suggested in the studyguide.

11. Some questions are marked with a ⟁. This indicates that further information is available in the Leader's Notes at the back of the guide.

12. For further information on getting a new Bible study group started and keeping it functioning effectively, read Gladys Hunt's *You Can Start a Bible Study Group* and *Pilgrims in Progress: Growing through Groups* by Jim and Carol Plueddemann (both available from Shaw Books).

Suggestions for Group Members

1. Learn and apply the following ground rules for effective Bible study. (If new members join the group later, review these guidelines with the whole group.)

2. Remember that your goal is to learn all that you can *from the Bible passage being studied.* Let it speak for itself without using Bible commentaries or other Bible passages. There is more than enough in each assigned passage to keep your group productively occupied for one session. Sticking to the passage saves the group from insecurity ("I don't have the right reference books—or the time to read anything else.") and confusion ("Where did that come from? I thought we were studying _____.").

3. Avoid the temptation to bring up those fascinating tangents that don't really grow out of the passage you are discussing. If the topic is of common interest, you can bring it up later in informal conversation after the study. Meanwhile, help one another stick to the subject.

4. Encourage one another to participate. People remember best what they discover and verbalize for

themselves. Some people are naturally shy, while others may be afraid of making a mistake. If your discussion is free and friendly and you show real interest in what group members think and feel, the quieter ones will be more likely to speak up. Remember, the more people involved in a discussion, the richer it will be.

5. Guard yourself from answering too many questions or talking too much. Give others a chance to share their ideas. If you are one who participates easily, discipline yourself by counting to ten before you open your mouth!

6. Make personal, honest applications and commit yourself to letting God's Word change you.

Wisdom for Today's Woman

*H*ave you ever noticed how curious we human beings are about other people's lives? From magazines devoted to people and television programs showing us how the rich and famous live to biographies giving graphic details, we devour information about how other people live—their choices and habits, their experiences and dreams.

God in his wisdom knows all about our fascination with how people live and what makes them tick. He also knows that we learn from example. So in the Bible, God hasn't just given us a book of doctrine as a means to knowing him. As the Master Teacher, he's given us an incredible variety of stories about regular people and how they handled the various circumstances they faced. In this way, we see not only who God is, but how he is involved in our lives.

The book of Esther is one example of such a story. In fact, God's name is not even mentioned in its pages, nor is any doctrine taught. But his presence is evident, and his power and care are obvious as he works behind the scenes to rescue his people, the Jews.

The story of Esther begins not with her, but with King Xerxes, Queen Vashti, and the king's advisor, Memucan. All three reacted to circumstances in ways that can teach us lessons for our own lives. We then meet Mordecai and Esther, descendants of those Jews who had been taken into captivity approximately one hundred years earlier because of God's judgment on their idolatry.

Mordecai adopted Esther and raised her to honor and serve God. Both her outer and inner beauty were critical factors in God's plan to use her to save his people from destruction. She goes into the king's palace as a young virgin who has never been exposed to the lifestyle of women taken into a heathen court and kept for the pleasure of the king. She emerges a woman of wisdom, strength, and courage, but not without going through much difficulty and great testing of her faith— the same process God employs today to shape us into women he can use.

From the introduction of Haman and onward, this story equals the best thrillers written today. Puffed up with pride and pettiness, emboldened by power and fueled by prejudice, Haman is an ugly character. Yet, if we are wise, we'll find lessons and warnings for ourselves even from him.

The apostle Paul wrote, "All Scripture is God-breathed and is useful for teaching, rebuking, correcting and training in righteousness" (2 Timothy 3:16). The book of Esther definitely teaches us, through both negative and positive examples, how to become wiser women for living in today's ever-changing world.

Choices Have Consequences

ESTHER 1

*W*omen today have more choices than ever before in history. We can choose to marry or stay single. We can pursue higher education, climb a career ladder, or run for political office. As we make choices, we need to realize that even the little ones repeated day in and day out lead us along certain paths, determining the course of our lives and defining the kind of people we will be. If we are wise, we also know that our choices often have consequences that seriously affect others as well.

The same was true in ancient times. As the book of Esther opens, we are introduced to wealthy King Xerxes and his lovely queen, Vashti. We'll see that even royalty can make hasty and unwise choices that have far-reaching consequences.

1. Think of a time when you made a quick decision without really considering the consequences. What was the result?

Read Esther 1:1-12.

᠕2. What details do you learn about Xerxes here (verses 1-3)?

3. Based on this opening passage, what is your initial impression of the king and queen?

---

᠕ *Indicates further information in Leader's Notes*

4. Describe the scene at the banquet: How long did it last? Who was invited? What was the mood? Where was Queen Vashti?

What was the purpose of this lavish party?

5. Describe the decision Xerxes made on the seventh day of the party (verses 10-11). Why do you think he acted in this way?

6. What negative influences sometimes affect your decision making?

7. Why do you think Queen Vashti made the choice she did?

READ ESTHER 1:13-22.

✒8. What was Memucan's counsel to Xerxes?

9. What assumptions fueled Memucan's advice (verses 16-20)?

How would you summarize his attitude?

10. List all the consequences that Xerxes—and others—faced because of his hasty edict.

11. In his role as royal advisor, Memucan had great influence over Xerxes. What attitudes and qualities characterize those you look to for advice?

12. What choices—big or small—are you facing now that will affect others?

What insights from this study can help you make wise choices?

Responding Wisely

ESTHER 2

*T*he news devastated my friend Jan. Her college sweetheart, husband, and father of their two preschoolers had died in a plane crash. Over the next twenty years Jan turned to God for guidance in raising her sons, for courage to face breast cancer, for strength to help her parents cope with Alzheimer's disease, and for wisdom for numerous other life crises. How has Jan survived without sinking into self-pity, resentment, or bitterness? She chooses to respond wisely rather than impetuously to each new situation. She chooses to believe God is good no matter what comes her way.

Long before a crisis turns our world upside down, our character is being formed. When trouble comes, our real character with all its strengths and weaknesses is displayed. More importantly, the depth of our relationship with God is also revealed. In this study, we will look at the responses of Xerxes

and Esther to the difficult situations in which they found
themselves. They faced different struggles and chose different
solutions. But through the choices they made, both revealed
their true characters.

   1. Do you agree with the statement "Circumstances
don't cause our character; they reveal it"? Why or
why not?

READ ESTHER 2:1-18.

*History records that, after the gathering of his military officers and
political leaders described in chapter 1, Xerxes went to war with
Greece and was defeated in 480 B.C. He returned to Persia and
Esther became queen in 479.*

   2. What kinds of emotions might Xerxes have experienced following the loss of Vashti and the battle
against Greece?

3. Why do you think the attendants proposed that the king find a new queen (verses 2-4)?

What similar advice do people struggling with unfulfilled emotional needs receive from society today?

4. What do the attendants' proposal and Xerxes' reaction to their suggestion tell you about the way women were viewed in that day?

5. How had Mordecai, a Jew, ended up in Susa (verses 5-6)?

What was his response to the alien circumstances in which he found himself?

6. Describe the qualities you see in Mordecai (verses 7-11).

   What kind of influence would he have had on Esther's character?

7. Note the details we learn about Esther's background. What are your first impressions of this young girl?

8. Once taken into the palace, what were Esther's circumstances and prospects?

What phrase is repeated in verses 9, 15, and 17? What does that phrase reveal about Esther's attitude to circumstances she never chose to be in?

9. What attitudes *could* Esther have chosen, given her possible future as a concubine, forced to live in a harem for life?

What can you learn and apply to your life from Esther's responses to her difficult situation?

Read Esther 2:19-23.

10. Note Mordecai's instruction to Esther in verse 20. Why do you think he told her to do this?

11. What did Mordecai do when he discovered a plot against the king?

What do Mordecai's actions reveal about his character?

12. What tends to be your initial response to tough or unfair circumstances?

What steps can you take to help you trust God and respond more wisely?

Pride and Pettiness

ESTHER 3

When I join a small Bible study group, my instinctive habit is to size up the people and see if they have anything worthwhile to say to me. Is this pride?" Linda asked me with an embarrassed laugh. Whether it's feeling superior by quietly comparing your intellect to others or loudly putting someone else down, pride and its ugly consequences have plagued the human heart since the beginning of time.

Being wise means being alert to our attitudes and motives. In addition to watching for pride, we need to be on the lookout for pettiness. How important is that issue you're fuming about anyway? Pettiness is magnifying the minor and ignoring the major—something that's easy to do in our roles as wives, mothers, colleagues, or friends. As we continue our study, Esther is now queen and her cousin Mordecai is well known in the court. But all is not well in the kingdom. Human pride, pettiness, and power combine themselves into a lethal mix in the form of one person.

1. Author J. Oswald Sanders suggests the following three questions as a test for pride. What is my reaction when
   - someone else is asked to do something I expected to do?
   - someone else gets praise and I'm forgotten?
   - someone outshines me in his or her accomplishments?

   What insights about the nature of pride—your own pride—do you gain from these questions?

READ ESTHER 3:1-15.

2. Who are the main players in this scene?

3. Who was Haman (verses 1-2)? Why did everyone pay him honor?

4. From what you know about Mordecai up to this point, why do you think he refused to bow down to Haman?

5. Can you think of a modern-day situation in which a Christian might have to take a stand, as Mordecai did?

If you faced a similar conflict of conscience, what would you do? Why?

6. Why do you think Haman was so furious and determined to punish Mordecai (verses 5-6)?

How are Haman's inner attitudes revealed by his reaction?

7. How did Haman enlist the king's aid in his plot against the Jews (verses 7-11)?

What strategies do we sometimes use to persuade others to our point of view?

8. Describe aspects of Xerxes' character that are revealed through this incident (verses 10-11,15).

9. Steps were quickly taken to carry out Haman's request for revenge. Discuss the different reactions the king, the city, and the Jews had after the edict was sent out.

10. Look back at the "pride test" in question 1. Think about your positions in the workplace, home, community, or church. How do you usually expect people to treat you in each setting?

How do you feel and act when you don't receive the treatment you expect? (If you wish, just think about or write down your answers.)

11. We all act like Haman sometimes. Which sin do you tend to struggle with the most: pride, pettiness, racism, or the desire for revenge?

12. How can you begin to overcome the sins you just identified? What do you need to start or stop doing? Pray for grace and humility to trust God's way.

Fear or Faith?

ESTHER 4

The story is told of an atheist who was ill and bedridden. He had two sons. One day he asked the younger one to write on a chalkboard placed at the side of his bed. He was told to write: "God is nowhere." When the older son came into the room, his father asked him to read the statement aloud. The son read: "God is now here."

How do you respond to a sudden crisis? With consuming fear, feeling that God is nowhere to be found? Or with faith that God is there with you?

This study focuses on the responses of both Mordecai and Esther to the crisis that swept into their lives because of Haman's hatred. As they discovered, whatever our frightening situation, God hasn't left us to our own resources. He has provided his Word, his Spirit, and other believers to help us stand firm when our world is shaken.

1. When have you been encouraged by seeing someone else exhibit faith in a tough situation? Be specific in describing that person's response and how you were encouraged by it.

READ ESTHER 4:1-8.

2. How did Mordecai and the Jews react to the king's edict?

What range of emotions must they have felt?

3. Why do you think Esther responded to Mordecai's behavior as she did (verses 4-5)?

4. What did Mordecai tell Hathach? Why would he trust this information to one of the king's eunuchs?

READ ESTHER 4:9-17.

5. What does Esther's reply reveal about her initial feelings in this crisis (verses 10-11)?

Put yourself in Esther's shoes. How do you think you would respond to a crisis that threatens your life and those you love?

6. What do you learn about Mordecai's faith from his challenge to Esther?

7. How do you account for the change you see from Mordecai's first reaction to the edict to his confident assertion to Esther?

8. What impact did Mordecai's statement make on Esther (verses 13-16)?

9. Prayer usually accompanied fasting. Esther, the royal queen, asked the ordinary Jews in Susa to pray and fast with her. What does this act tell you about her character? her faith?

Why do we sometimes find it difficult to ask others to pray for us?

10. What was Esther seeking from God through fasting and prayer?

How have you been helped, or been given wisdom or guidance, by either prayer or fasting?

11. Review Mordecai's famous question to Queen Esther in verse 14. Have you ever sensed that God had you in a certain place for a particular purpose? What happened?

12. What positive changes occur in your life when your focus moves from fear to faith and trust in God?

Trials Are for Growing

ESTHER 5

*A*my Carmichael, a missionary to India, wrote: "Can he have followed far who has no wound, no scar?" Many Christ-followers seem surprised to find themselves going through a time of trial and suffering. Angry with God, doubting his love, and filled with self-pity, these individuals often overlook the opportunities their trials present.

The Bible leaves us in no doubt that some trials are part of living in a fallen world, while others come because of our faith in Christ. Whatever their source, every trial can be an instrument for blessing in God's loving purposes. "Consider it pure joy…whenever you face trials of many kinds," wrote James (1:2). Why? Because the testing of our faith develops perseverance, character, and hope. Esther discovered that trials are opportunities to get to know God better, to receive his wisdom, and to step out in faith and courage to do his will.

1. Recall a difficult trial you have been through. Looking back, how did your faith grow because of that experience?

READ ESTHER 5:1-8.

2. How many days did Esther wait before going to the king? What had occupied her time (4:15-16)?

3. When you face a tough decision, what can waiting—accompanied by prayer and/or fasting—accomplish?

4. Identify the emotions and thoughts Esther might have had as she stood in the inner court of the palace.

   What encouragement did she receive at the beginning of this difficult situation?

5. What plan of action did God give to Esther after she had waited on him for three days?

6. Even though the king obviously loved Esther, why do you think she didn't present her request immediately at the first banquet?

7. Have you ever felt that God has held you back from
    speaking out because it wasn't the right time? If so,
    what happened?

READ ESTHER 5:9-14.

8. What was Haman so happy about that day
    (verse 9)? What minor event spoiled his mood?

9. What aspects of prejudice do you observe in this
    passage?

10. How did Haman, his wife, and their friends justify their sense of superiority?

11. What principles seemed to guide Esther in this complex and difficult trial in her life?

12. How can you apply this wisdom to the trials you are facing now?

God Is in Control

Our study has focused on the human characters in the book of Esther, but the most important and powerful person in this story is never mentioned in its pages. God himself was watching this drama unfold and working to bring about the deliverance of the Jews. God saw and anticipated the crisis that befell his people. And long before it occurred, he was putting people into place so that his plan of deliverance would unfold in his perfect time.

The book of Esther clearly illustrates the providence of God. The word *providence* is derived from two words: *pro* meaning "before" and *video* meaning "I see." More than simply foresight, however, providence also means having the power to act ahead of time to meet an unseen need. Providence encompasses both divine *pre*-vision and *pro*-vision. Like Esther, the woman of wisdom trusts that God is in control—even when she can't see him at work.

1. When have you experienced God's providence in your life? Tell about it.

READ ESTHER 6.

2. Following Esther's first banquet, the king couldn't sleep. What was the result of his sleeplessness (verses 1-3)?

3. According to Esther 2:22-23, the king had been told of this event but had failed to honor Mordecai. What does the king's rediscovery of this fact tell you about both Mordecai and Esther?

4. The plot thickens as Haman enters to ask for Mordecai's death. Which of Haman's secret longings are revealed in his answer to the king (verses 6-9)?

5. What emotions and thoughts might Haman have wrestled with as events took an unexpected turn (verses 10-12)?

6. What lessons do you learn from Haman about the inherent dangers of seeking status and recognition for ourselves?

▼7. Someone has said, "When you stop praying, the 'coincidences' stop happening." Although God is not mentioned, list the ways you see him working through Xerxes.

8. Compare and contrast Haman's and Mordecai's attitudes and responses to being honored by the king.

9. Why is it important to maintain an accurate and humble assessment of ourselves?

10. How do the events in this chapter encourage you to trust both God's timing and his ways?

11. How might you live differently if you really believed and trusted in God's providence?

Sowing and Reaping

ESTHER 7–8

Lingering outside my daughter's closed bedroom door, I listened as she instructed her dolls, Heather and Sherrie, on how to behave. I found myself alternately amused and alarmed. The very words and tone of voice I had used toward her were not only sown deeply in her little mind, but they also were bearing fruit! Sowing and reaping don't just apply to planting corn and tomatoes or raising children. It's a principle that applies to all of life.

After persuading Xerxes to write a decree condemning the Jews to death, Haman had sought one more favor from the king. It was not to be. The tide had turned. After being forced to honor Mordecai on the king's behalf, Haman was now summoned to attend Esther's second banquet. He would soon discover, at great cost, a principle of life every wise woman also bears in mind: We will reap what we sow.

1. Discuss a "sowing" situation in your life or in someone else's life that has yielded negative consequences or positive consequences.

READ ESTHER 7.

2. In what ways did Esther's situation change between the first and second banquets?

3. Describe the way Esther presented her case.

What impresses you about her handling of this situation?

4. What might have happened if Esther had spoken against Haman earlier?

5. How does this story illustrate the truth found in Galatians 6:7-8?

READ ESTHER 8.

6. What did Esther reveal about herself and her relationship to Mordecai (verse 1)?

From the king's perspective, why would this connection strengthen her case?

7. Describe Esther's primary concern after Haman was hanged (verses 3-8).

8. Look again at Esther 3:8-10 in light of chapter 8. How do you account for the king's change of heart concerning his earlier decree?

9. How were the Jewish people helped by the king's new edict (verses 11-13)? (Compare with 3:13.)

Why was this new edict necessary?

10. Identify the character qualities you saw in Esther as she pleaded for her people.

    Which of these would you like to see developed in your life?

11. How did Mordecai, like Haman, reap what he had sown?

    What encouragement does Mordecai's story give you in a difficult situation you face?

12. When have you seen God turn around a seemingly impossible situation in your life or someone else's life?

What does this example show you about God?

Shaped by God for a Purpose

ESTHER 9–10

*A*s a woman in midlife I sometimes find myself think-ing, *I wish I had known years ago some of what I know today.* What am I wishing for? Wisdom! In his book *Knowing God,* J. I. Packer defines wisdom as "the power to see, and the inclination to choose the best and highest goal, together with the surest means of attaining it." This definition accurately depicts the way both Esther and Mordecai acted in a time of deadly peril.

As we come to the end of the book of Esther, we see God bringing two ordinary people into a place of great responsibil-ity and prominence. Nothing of Mordecai's and Esther's earlier experiences was wasted, and no expression of their dedication to the Lord went unnoticed. All of it contributed to God's purpose. And when the hour came for them to stand for him, Mordecai and Esther didn't fail. God's ways of developing people he can use haven't changed, nor have his purposes. Be encouraged! He is shaping your character and capabilities through various experiences—both happy and heartbreaking —so you can attain wisdom and serve him in your home, workplace, community, and church.

1. Spend a few minutes reflecting on your life up to the present. Is there a particular person or event that God has used to shape who you are today? Explain.

READ ESTHER 9:1-19.

2. How had the situation changed for the Jews throughout Xerxes' empire (verses 1-4)?

Why were the officials fearful of Mordecai?

3. What did the Jews do in response to the king's new edict?

What differences do you find between the events in Susa and the rest of Xerxes' kingdom (verses 13-18)?

4. What significant phrase do you find repeated after each assault by the Jews?

What does this phrase reveal about the Jews' motives and attitudes in this situation?

❧5. Why do you think Esther made the request found in verse 13?

READ ESTHER 9:20-32.

6. Describe the specific instructions Mordecai gave the Jews after their deliverance.

7. Why was it important for the Jews to establish and observe the feast of Purim?

8. What has God done in your life that you can celebrate?

What do you do to keep this memory alive in your heart and mind?

READ ESTHER 10.

9. What further honors did Mordecai receive from
   Xerxes? (See also 8:1-2,7-10,15; 9:3-4,20-22,
   29-32.)

   How did he use his new position of power?

10. Reflect on Mordecai's and Esther's difficult experi-
    ences throughout their lives. How did God use these
    tough times to shape them into the kind of people
    he could use?

What encouragement for your own life do you find in Mordecai and Esther's experiences?

11. Think back over the story of Esther. What evidence have you seen of God's involvement in this drama?

12. What practical wisdom or encouragement for your daily life have you gleaned from this study of Esther?

Leader's Notes

Study 1: Choices Have Consequences

Question 2. Xerxes reigned from 486–465 B.C. His Greek name was Ahasuerus. His kingdom extended from modern-day Iran (Persia) to Ethiopia (Cush). Historians record that he was unpredictable, powerful, and violent.

Question 4. Nehemiah, who served in Susa thirty years after these events, records that both the king and queen sat on their thrones together (Nehemiah 2:6). In Esther we see King Xerxes and Queen Vashti entertaining men and women separately. The king had absolute authority and could choose to have his wife by his side or hidden away. To defy his command to come before him, or to appear without invitation, was to risk death.

Question 8. The law of the Medes and Persians meant that even the king could not cancel a decree he had sent out. There was no room for second thoughts! Only a further decree could offset the effects of the first, but the original command could never be reversed.

Study 2: Responding Wisely

Question 4. Women were considered property and had no rights. If they were chosen for the king's pleasure, they could not refuse to obey him. Once taken from their homes, they were housed in a separate building—a harem—next to the palace. Each spent one night with the king. After this, all the women, along with whoever was chosen queen, would spend the rest of their lives together, guarded by eunuchs (men who had been castrated).

Question 5. The Jews had been taken into captivity approximately one hundred years before the events recorded in Esther (2 Kings 25). Two groups had gone back to Jerusalem, one under Zerubbabel and one under Ezra (Ezra 1:2–2:2; 7). However, many stayed where they had been resettled. Perhaps some feared the long and dangerous journey back. Others had established new lives and were reluctant to begin again in the devastated country of their ancestors.

Study 3: Pride and Pettiness

Question 1. Bulleted questions taken from *Spiritual Leadership* by J. Oswald Sanders (Chicago: Moody Press, 1967), p. 143.

Question 3. Haman was an Agagite, a descendant of the ancient rulers of the Amalekites, Israel's sworn enemies. Exodus 17:8-16 recounts the famous battle that raged between Israel and the Amalekites during which Moses held up his arms in prayer. Deuteronomy 25:17-19 reminds the Israelites of their godless enemy and commands them to "blot out the memory of Amalek," which they failed to do. King Saul's later disobedience to this command from God ultimately led to his downfall (1 Samuel 15).

Question 7. Casting lots was a common way to make decisions in the ancient world. Dice or other tokens may have been used to remove human choice from the decision. Aaron cast lots in choosing the goat for the sin offering (Leviticus 16:8-10). Joshua cast lots before the Lord to assign portions of land to the tribes (Joshua 18:6-10). Counting on the "lot"—*pur* in Persian—to determine the best day for attacking the Jews, Haman had to settle for a day nearly a year later. This ensured plenty of time for God to work through his chosen agents.

STUDY 4: FEAR OR FAITH?

Question 2. Both sackcloth (clothes worn as a symbol of mourning) and ashes were a visible sign of overwhelming grief. Job tore his clothes and sat in ashes (Job 1:20; 2:8); Daniel pleaded with the Lord for his people "in prayer and petition, in fasting, and in sackcloth and ashes" (Daniel 9:3). Sackcloth and ashes also represented heartfelt repentance (Jonah 3:5-6; Matthew 11:21).

Question 9. Fasting usually implies going without food for a specific time and purpose. It can include abstaining from any regular activity in order to focus more clearly on seeking God's presence. Fasting was mandatory for the Jewish people once a year, on the Day of Atonement. Going without food or other "necessities" reminds us of our total dependence on God for every need. Accompanied by prayer, fasting can be an activity that draws us closer to God and allows him to have our full attention.

STUDY 5: TRIALS ARE FOR GROWING

Question 3. Waiting on the Lord is a common theme in Scripture. (See Psalms 27:14; 33:20; 40:1.) God uses times of waiting to help us mature in our faith, to put his plans into action, and to give needed wisdom and direction.

Question 9. You may want to guide your group in discussing the meaning of *prejudice* and *racism,* both of which characterize Haman's attitude toward the Jews. *Prejudice* is having a superior attitude toward others, forgetting that God is the Creator of all and that Jesus Christ died to redeem people from every nation and language group. *Racism* looks at the outside of people, comparing, judging, rejecting. God looks on the heart and calls us to reflect his love to others. Haman hated a whole group of people because of their different customs and beliefs. His story serves as a warning to all of us.

STUDY 6: GOD IS IN CONTROL

Question 3. The discovery of the plot against the king occurred before Haman was elevated to second in the kingdom and began his vendetta against Mordecai. It was a serious oversight on the part of Xerxes not to have honored Mordecai as he was never to be indebted to any of his subjects. When it came to his remembrance, he acted immediately.

Question 7. God's providence is seen in the timing of Xerxes' sleeplessness, his choice of reading matter, and his sense of urgency to put right this oversight of honoring Mordecai who had saved his life. The timing of Haman's appearance and his involvement in determining Mordecai's reward further reveals God's power to carry out his will regardless of the forces arrayed against him. (See also Job 42:2; Isaiah 14:24,27; 46:10.)

Question 9. You may want to ask the group to define *humility* in the context of this book and its characters. Think back to question 3 and Mordecai's humility; think about Esther's humble approach to the king, etc.

STUDY 7: SOWING AND REAPING

Question 2. Have the group look back through the book and review the timing of the events. Mordecai appealed to Esther the day he heard about the decree to kill the Jews. Three days later, Esther went before the king inviting him and Haman to a banquet that day. She invited them back for a second banquet the next day. In the twenty-four hours of Esther 6, between the first and second banquets, God turned the situation upside down. Mordecai, Esther, and the Jewish people found their destiny completely changed *in five days.*

Question 9. Esther and Mordecai were allowed to write a decree enabling the Jews to assemble and protect themselves on the very same day in which the first edict declared they were to be plundered and killed. Under the first edict the Israelites were helpless victims of their neighbors; under the second they could kill any who might attack them.

STUDY 8: SHAPED BY GOD FOR A PURPOSE

Question 4. If the Jews had sought to take material advantage of their enemies, they could have done so. Plundering your enemies was the common practice in ancient warfare. (See Genesis 14:8-12 and Joshua 8:27.) The Jews fought only to protect themselves and their families, not to enrich themselves or take advantage of their new status.

Question 5. Scholars have differing views on why Esther asked for the extra day. "We have no means of knowing the exact situation.... The purpose of hanging the dead bodies of Haman's sons would be to let all Susa know their fate" (J. G. Baldwin, *The New Bible Commentary: Revised,* Grand Rapids, Mich.: Eerdmans, 1970, p. 419).

Question 7. Mordecai gave detailed instructions for the feast of Purim. To this day, Jews around the world commemorate God's powerful deliverance of their people through Esther. At the end of the joyful celebration, which has been kept for some 2,500 years, the book of Esther is read in the synagogue and people hiss and spit when the name of Haman is mentioned!

What Should We Study Next?

To help your group answer that question, we've listed the Fisherman Studyguides by category so you can choose your next study.

TOPICAL STUDIES

Angels by Vinita Hampton Wright

Becoming Women of Purpose by Ruth Haley Barton

Building Your House on the Lord: Marriage and Parenthood by Steve and Dee Brestin

The Creative Heart of God: Living with Imagination by Ruth Goring

Discipleship: The Growing Christian's Lifestyle by James and Martha Reapsome

Doing Justice, Showing Mercy: Christian Actions in Today's World by Vinita Hampton Wright

Encouraging Others: Biblical Models for Caring by Lin Johnson

The End Times: Discovering What the Bible Says by E. Michael Rusten

Examining the Claims of Jesus by Dee Brestin

Friendship: Portraits in God's Family Album by Steve and Dee Brestin

The Fruit of the Spirit: Growing in Christian Character by Stuart Briscoe

Great Doctrines of the Bible by Stephen Board

Great Passages of the Bible by Carol Plueddemann

Great Prayers of the Bible by Carol Plueddemann

Growing Through Life's Challenges by James and Martha
   Reapsome

Guidance & God's Will by Tom and Joan Stark

Heart Renewal: Finding Spiritual Refreshment by Ruth
   Goring

Higher Ground: Steps Toward Christian Maturity by Steve
   and Dee Brestin

*Images of Redemption: God's Unfolding Plan Through the
   Bible* by Ruth Van Reken

Integrity: Character from the Inside Out by Ted Engstrom
   and Robert Larson

Lifestyle Priorities by John White

Marriage: Learning from Couples in Scripture by R. Paul
   and Gail Stevens

Miracles by Robbie Castleman

One Body, One Spirit: Building Relationships in the Church
   by Dale and Sandy Larsen

The Parables of Jesus by Gladys Hunt

Parenting with Purpose and Grace by Alice Fryling

Prayer: Discovering What the Bible Says by Timothy Jones
   and Jill Zook-Jones

The Prophets: God's Truth Tellers by Vinita Hampton
   Wright

Proverbs and Parables: God's Wisdom for Living by Dee
   Brestin

Satisfying Work: Christian Living from Nine to Five
   by R. Paul Stevens and Gerry Schoberg

Senior Saints: Growing Older in God's Family by James and
   Martha Reapsome

The Sermon on the Mount: The God Who Understands Me
    by Gladys Hunt
Spiritual Gifts by Karen Dockrey
Spiritual Hunger: Filling Your Deepest Longings by Jim and
    Carol Plueddemann
A Spiritual Legacy: Faith for the Next Generation by Chuck
    and Winnie Christensen
Spiritual Warfare by A. Scott Moreau
The Ten Commandments: God's Rules for Living by Stuart
    Briscoe
Ultimate Hope for Changing Times by Dale and Sandy
    Larsen
Who Is God? by David P. Seemuth
Who Is Jesus? In His Own Words by Ruth Van Reken
Who Is the Holy Spirit? by Barbara Knuckles and Ruth Van
    Reken
Wisdom for Today's Woman: Insights from Esther by Poppy
    Smith
Witnesses to All the World: God's Heart for the Nations
    by Jim and Carol Plueddemann
Women at Midlife: Embracing the Challenges by Jeanie
    Miley
Worship: Discovering What Scripture Says by Larry Sibley

BIBLE BOOK STUDIES

Genesis: Walking with God by Margaret Fromer and
    Sharrel Keyes
Exodus: God Our Deliverer by Dale and Sandy Larsen
Ezra and Nehemiah: A Time to Rebuild by James Reapsome

(For Esther, see Topical Studies, *Wisdom for Today's Woman*)
Job: Trusting Through Trials by Ron Klug
Psalms: A Guide to Prayer and Praise by Ron Klug
Proverbs: Wisdom That Works by Vinita Hampton Wright
Ecclesiastes: A Time for Everything by Stephen Board
Jeremiah: The Man and His Message by James Reapsome
Jonah, Habakkuk, and Malachi: Living Responsibly
    by Margaret Fromer and Sharrel Keyes
Matthew: People of the Kingdom by Larry Sibley
Mark: God in Action by Chuck and Winnie Christensen
Luke: Following Jesus by Sharrel Keyes
John: The Living Word by Whitney Kuniholm
Acts 1–12: God Moves in the Early Church by Chuck and
    Winnie Christensen
Acts 13–28, see *Paul* under Character Studies
Romans: The Christian Story by James Reapsome
1 Corinthians: Problems and Solutions in a Growing Church
    by Charles and Ann Hummel
Strengthened to Serve: 2 Corinthians by Jim and Carol
    Plueddemann
Galatians, Titus, and Philemon: Freedom in Christ
    by Whitney Kuniholm
Ephesians: Living in God's Household by Robert Baylis
Philippians: God's Guide to Joy by Ron Klug
Colossians: Focus on Christ by Luci Shaw
Letters to the Thessalonians by Margaret Fromer and Sharrel
    Keyes
Letters to Timothy: Discipleship in Action by Margaret
    Fromer and Sharrel Keyes
Hebrews: Foundations for Faith by Gladys Hunt
James: Faith in Action by Chuck and Winnie Christensen

1 and 2 Peter, Jude: Called for a Purpose by Steve and Dee
    Brestin
How Should a Christian Live? 1, 2, and 3 John by Dee
    Brestin
Revelation: The Lamb Who Is a Lion by Gladys Hunt

BIBLE CHARACTER STUDIES

Abraham: Model of Faith by James Reapsome
David: Man After God's Own Heart by Robbie Castleman
Elijah: Obedience in a Threatening World by Robbie
    Castleman
Great People of the Bible by Carol Plueddemann
King David: Trusting God for a Lifetime by Robbie
    Castleman
Men Like Us: Ordinary Men, Extraordinary God by Paul
    Heidebrecht and Ted Scheuermann
Moses: Encountering God by Greg Asimakoupoulos
Paul: Thirteenth Apostle (Acts 13–28) by Chuck and
    Winnie Christensen
Women Like Us: Wisdom for Today's Issues by Ruth Haley
    Barton
Women Who Achieved for God by Winnie Christensen
Women Who Believed God by Winnie Christensen